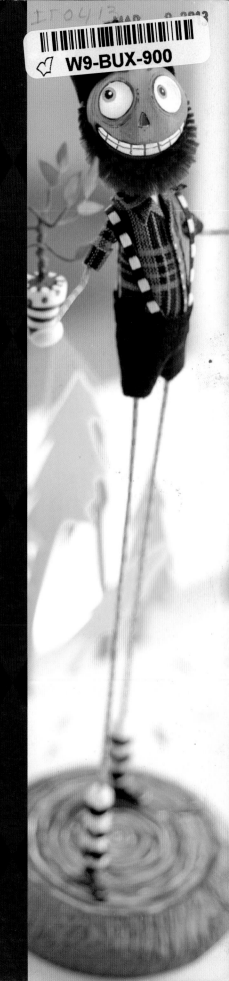

GLITTERVILLE'S
Handmade Halloween

GLITTERVILLE'S

HANDMADE
HALLOWEEN

A GLITTERED GUIDE FOR WHIMSICAL CRAFTING!

STEPHEN BROWN

Andrews McMeel
Publishing, LLC
Kansas City • Sydney • London

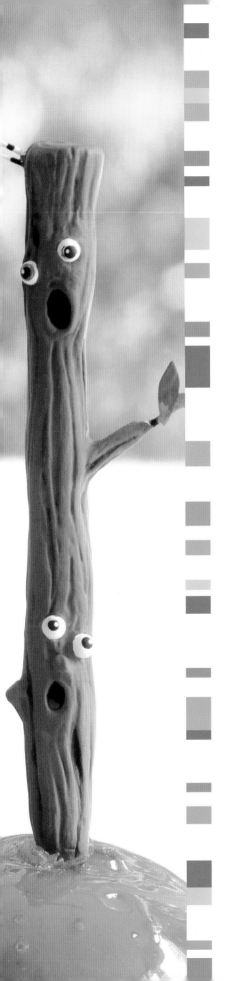

Contents

Acknowledgments vi
Introduction viii
Glitter Guide x

Cellophane Fancies 1
Buckets of Fun 9
Paper Festooning 15
Oh-So-Wicked! Party Hat 19
Chenille Pumpkins 35
Halloween Candy Garland 43
ButterScream Frosting Ornament 51
Nut Cups 61
Pinky's Pumpkin Patch 67
Mushroom Man on a Stump 75
Wacky Willie Webber Spider Puppet 83
Lumber Jack 91
Spooky Forest Sticks and Orange Candy Apples 105
Party Hat Place Card Holders 117
Glittered Cat Silhouette Party Hat 123
Harvest Moon Halloween Hanger 129
Kooky Cupcake Picks 135
Pumpkin Tiara 141
The Bride of Franky GlitterStein 149
Trick or Tweet 161

Patterns, Templates and Banner Art 168

I would also like to thank my literary agent Coleen O'Shea . . . who in my book is more than OK!

Susan Wilson
Christi Clemons Hoffman
Julie Barnes
Holly Ogden
Editor of the Year! Lane Butler

BRYAN

Above all, I must thank my friend and assistant Bryan "Chico" Crabtree for his undeterred devotion in helping me create this book and for making every project look magical through his camera lens!

In the STUDIO
Mark Howard
Lynn Shepherd

ACKNOWLEDGMENTS

Mary Lynn Campbell

Bill Black

Marianne Custer

Janis Johnson

Anita Donofrio

Anne Powers

Making every day a holiday takes more than just glitter and glue,
but how it all happens most have not a clue
that there are lots of enablers behind "Make and Do"!

Special thanks to all my friends who have made
Glitterville a part of their lives over the years—even when
that little voice inside of them clearly said "Run"!

Ann Knight
Sandra Herrera
Myra Green
Carole Oliver
Jean Bardorf
Bryan Wilkerson
Rachel Parton
Sarah Mee
Karen Nickell

Willie & Patricia Brown ✳ John & Enza Cline
Thanks to my parents and grandparents for allowing me to run with scissors and all
the other necessary supplies needed to bring my glittered world to life!

Ann Baker · Nell Brown · Jeff, Karen & Aaron Crabtree · Jonathan Crouch · David Dewey
Erin Donovan · Ron Emery · Tracy Griffith · Brenda Howard · Vickers Johnson · Allen Knight · Laurel McCall
Sharon Mioduch · Matt Mullins · Nancy Parrish · Fred & Nanita Samuels · Katie Wood · Valarie Woods

INTRODUCTION

For those of us who love the holidays and crafting, there is no time of the year more magical than Halloween. Although this autumnal festival is seen by some as a dark and spooky day, in Glitterville, it's a playground for colorful characters and projects dedicated to the sugary celebration of cupcakes, costumes, and all the candy you can eat!

My obsession for make and do has been lifelong! As a boy, I constantly found myself in post-holiday doldrums after every big celebration, until I learned that through crafting for the next upcoming occasion I could turn those feelings around and literally "Make every day a holiday!", the premise that I used to turn my kitchen crafts into a worldwide company.

Since Glitterville's beginning, I have been asked to share my secrets for making whimsically wacky creations, but I've been so busy crafting that I just haven't had time to do it—until now!

I can finally add to my craft repertoire making this book, *Glitterville's Handmade Halloween*, with all the tips, tricks, and techniques needed for making your holiday sparkle and shine using full-color how-tos and stories that rhyme!

My philosophy for crafting is the same as for cooking: simple ingredients make the best cake—or in this case, bats, cats, and party hats!

I don't believe your creativity should ever be limited to the number of fancy craft supplies you can afford, which is why all the projects in this book are made from easily acquired, basic materials, which are completely defined in a section called Stephen Brown's Glitter Guide: A Manual for Make & Do.

The pages of this book are filled with projects for making some of Glitterville's most beloved items, including Candy Garland that's perfect for hanging over your door, treat buckets, costumes, and oh, so much more! I even reveal my most sought after how-to of all, making folk art figures that celebrate fall.

So grab some glitter and be on your way to make it—and "Make every day a holiday!"

Stephen Brown's
GLITTER GUIDE
A Manual for Make & Do!

The number of craft supplies available in today's market can be overwhelming to new or experienced crafters alike. Beautiful packaging and the promise of their superior performance entices us to buy expensive tools and materials that just aren't necessary for leading a full and productive craft life.

My friends often tease that Glitterville was started from only a handful of Styrofoam balls, some chunky glitter, and a little white glue—and it's completely true!

Mastering the art of make and do means simply learning to create anything you want from only a few basic materials, tools you have at home, and simple techniques!

Before you start your new creations, read my crafting declarations and let the glitter guide your way to make every day a holiday!

Before starting any new project, the first thing I do is reach for a pencil and paper, in order to do a basic sketch of what I'm about to create. This process not only helps me envision what my finished craft may look like, it also allows me to think about the materials I might use and the project's basic construction. Keep in mind that this design doodle is not the finished product and doesn't have to be a work of art. It's simply a roadmap to your destination craft!

MATERIALS

Making magic for the holidays and every day doesn't require carts full of craft supplies . . . only a handful of talented basic materials. Although there are no hard-and-fast rules, I've divided the materials into three categories describing the role they play in most projects.

Structure
Materials used for building the base of a project

Style
Materials used for defining the look of a project

Sparkle
Materials used for giving your project that extra finishing touch

Structure

▪ PAPERCLAY

One of the most important materials on your craft table is some sort of sculpting clay. This allows you to create your own original elements for a project, such as heads, hands, and so on, instead of buying premade pieces. Mixing sculpted clay elements with other kinds of materials, such as paper and glitter, will give your work a truly one-of-a-kind look.

After trying almost every sculpting material on the market, ranging from polymer clays that require oven baking, to messy and hard-to-mix instant papier-mâché, I have found what I consider to be the ultimate clay for crafting. It's called Paperclay. Its texture is like a paper pulp; it's easily sculpted, holds fine detail, and air-dries to an ultra hard, sandable finish. It's inexpensive and can be purchased at most craft stores, or ordered wholesale direct from the company in large or small amounts. Paperclay is used in many of my projects, but you can use any sculptable clay material instead.

▪ STYROFOAM

Nothing makes creating a lightweight form for sculpting upon better than Styrofoam. It's found in basic shapes, from various sizes of balls to sheets and cones. It can be cut with a serrated kitchen knife, and pieces can be combined and attached together to make practically any shape imaginable.

It's very important to remember when building a structure from Styrofoam, that glue is not very helpful in holding it together. White glue is too slow to stick and has little effect on the porous material, and hot glue melts the Styrofoam completely. The best technique for joining pieces of Styrofoam together and making the structure much stronger is with round toothpicks.

Styrofoam usually comes in standard white and green. I prefer the white for aesthetic reasons but there is absolutely no difference between the makeup of the two. Do not confuse green Styrofoam with a floral foam called Oasis; this is a completely different material and will not work for our projects.

Packing Styrofoam can also be recycled for crafting, but tends to have a slick surface that's not as friendly to cutting and shaping. I save every scrap of Styrofoam, large or small, just in case it's needed for a future project.

▪ CARDBOARD

There are many different weights and varieties of cardboard, available at art supply stores as well as all around the house.

Poster board is a really lightweight cardboard that has a slick, clean surface, rolls easily, and is the perfect material for making cones for party hats.

Chipboard is made from recycled and compressed paper and comes in many different thicknesses. It's available in large and small sheets at art or craft supply stores. Its advantages over other cardboards is usually its weight and the ability to bond to itself very quickly with white glue. It paints without warping or wrinkling and is durable enough to be sanded on the edges to soften its rigidness.

Found boards are types of cardboard that are found and recycled from around the home. Many of my projects require cardboard tubes, and while I would like to pretend that I go to the cardboard tube store for those, in reality I usually go to the kitchen and try to free the tube from the still-full roll of paper towels. You can also use rolls from toilet tissue and wrapping paper. So to avoid the frenzy of leaving your paper products in a heap, save any empty tubes from whatever source available.

Other found boards include packing cardboards and the back of things such as your morning cereal box.

Materials

■ Card Stock

Many crafts require small bits of paper to be used for details such as wings, ears, or banners. Instead of using scrapbook papers that I may or may not have on my craft table, I use plain white 110-pound card stock and paint it with acrylics to get the color I need. Another benefit of this process is that the paper "wings" will match the painted sculpted body exactly. Card stock is inexpensive, completely versatile for sketching or crafting, and available in large packages alongside standard copy paper.

■ Glue

While adhesives are considered by some to be a sticky subject, for me it's pretty straightforward. Sometimes the more basic a material is, the better it is, and I have found this to be true with glue! Almost anything I make can be stuck together with either white glue or hot glue.

White glue is good for adhering paper, holding glitter in place, and any task not requiring instant stick. If you change your mind within a few minutes on where something is placed, it's likely you can pull it apart and reposition it.

Hot glue is great for instant glueification. It will hold the seam of a cardboard cone firmly shut, stick the fur of a marabou strand to a glittered surface, and perform many other tasks quickly. Its downsides are that it's immediately permanent, which can be a good or bad thing, it completely wrecks the surface of the item it's glued to, it's often messy, with lots of unsightly strings, and it has the ability to give you blisters if you get it on your fingers—which I have done oh so many times!

Many projects require a combination of white and hot glues, so keep both on your table and you will not get stuck!

■ Gesso

Gesso is useful to have but not absolutely necessary. It's best known for being used as the primer for stretched artists' canvas. Gesso resembles white paint but has the thickness and some of the properties of a wet plaster of Paris. It can be applied with a brush in different directions onto a surface needing texture, or used as filler on a surface you want to be smooth and free of cracks.

Once it's dry, gesso has a sandable surface and accepts paint easily. One large container will last most crafters a really long time. Its price ranges from inexpensive to pricey, depending on the brand. For general crafting, I go with the less expensive.

■ WIRE

When you need a piece of wire, nothing else will do! There are many sizes and types of this bendable material available, but for my projects I use floral wire, which is inexpensive and available at craft stores.

It comes packaged perfectly straight and is precut to a standard 18-inch length. Its thickness is listed by gauge. The smaller the number, the thicker the wire; the higher the number, the thinner the wire, which can be a confusing system to creative people like myself.

I tend to use only a few gauges:

★ 16-gauge is the strongest and perfect for making such things as arms and legs.
★ 18-gauge is sturdy but flexible enough to be bent into freeform shapes.
★ 20-gauge to 32-gauge are very thin wires that are great for holding small paper banners or other small details.

When a project calls for a length of painted wire, it refers to wire that has been wrapped with floral tape and painted for that specific project (see page xxiv).

■ FLORAL TAPE

What looks like a flimsy roll of paper tape with limited stickiness is actually one of the most valuable supplies on my craft table. I use it to wrap lengths of wire to soften the harshness of the metal and prepare the surface for painting and striping. Without floral tape, it's almost impossible to get paint to stick permanently, and the uncoated wire will eventually rust onto the rest of your project.

The trick to using floral tape is understanding that its glue is released only when the tape is pulled.

■ DOWELS, SKEWERS, AND TOOTHPICKS

No craft table should be without this band of wooden wonders. They can be used as materials as well as tools. The simple ¼-inch wooden dowel like those sold in the bakery section of the craft store, for supporting wedding cakes, is the start of many projects including the body of my folk art figures, such as Lumber Jack (page 91).

Skewers, sold in the kitchen department for making kebabs, are useful as tools, and cupcake picks are useful for their original intended purpose.

The last in this trio is the toothpick, available in round and flat. I prefer round. These little helpful splinters are always there when you need them, from bringing Styrofoam pieces closer together, to serving as small flagpoles, to holding painted things to dry. If you have not yet discovered the joy of toothpicks, just set some on your craft table and you will quickly see everything there is to do with them.

■ WOODEN BALLS

Every craft store has an unfinished wood section with hundreds of little wooden doodads for crafting. Within that area are bags of small wooden balls ranging in size from less than ½ inch to several inches in diameter. They make perfect little heads for projects such as the Cellophane Fancies (page 1).

■ BOXES AND BUCKETS

In the past few years, papier-mâché boxes and buckets have become very popular with crafters. They are an unassuming brown paper bag on store shelves, but in the hands of a crafter they're quickly transformed into glittered goodness. Sculpted heads and toppers can easily be attached to them, using glue or wire.

■ MONOFILAMENT

Although most of the people I know call this material "fishing line," its correct name is monofilament. It's sold in different "test," referring to its strength, which allows you to buy one strong enough to hold the fish you are expecting to catch. Since we are expecting only to catch a few candies on our line, a 20-pound test will be just fine.

■ WIRE CUTTERS

A good pair of wire cutters is one of the most necessary tools needed for crafting. I want them to be industrial enough to cut through wires of different thicknesses, so I prefer the wire cutters found at the hardware store over those found in craft stores.

■ EASY CUTTING TOOL

This is by far the most exotic hand tool I own. It looks like a pair of pliers, but is actually used for cutting wooden dowels and skewers cleanly at any angle, without splintering the end. They are inexpensive and seem to hide in the model building section of the craft store. Don't sweat it if you don't have one. I didn't have one for years! Just use a small hacksaw instead.

■ SERRATED KITCHEN KNIFE

One of the most useful tools on your craft table comes from your dinner table. A basic serrated knife used for cutting bread or steak is perfect for cutting things that require a longer blade than the one found in a craft knife. This is my favorite tool for cutting Styrofoam.

Other Tools

■ NEEDLE-NOSE PLIERS

The benefit of these pointy pliers is their ability to curl the ends of wire around their rounded point. I buy these at the hardware store as well. They are also sold as jewelry pliers in craft stores.

■ CLAY SCULPTING TOOL

Although many commercial sculpting tools are available for working with clay, I find that household items such as toothpicks, skewers, and plastic forks often work just as well as a "real" tool.

Tools

■ DRILL

Many projects require you to drill a hole for attaching accessories and so forth. I use a standard household drill from the hardware store, equipped with a set of drill bits ranging from small to large.

■ PUNCHES

The task of cutting out dozens of small shapes from paper is done effortlessly with the aid of hand punches. Punches can be used in two very different ways. You can use them for cutting out shapes needed as a material, or as a tool for leaving a shaped opening in your paper, and sometimes both. Although they are available in practically every shape, I use a standard hole punch for making small uniform holes and various circle punches. I also use a small star punch for making the trim on the Oh-So-Wicked! Party Hat (page 19).

■ PAINTBRUSHES

Most of my projects require a small detail brush for the face, a medium-size round bristle brush, and slightly flat brushes of varying widths for painting larger areas. I prefer synthetic nylon bristles for craft work because of their sturdiness. Natural bristle brushes tend to shed and leave bristles in your paint.

■ SEWING TOOLS

Having a sewing machine on your craft table is great, but any projects in this book requiring stitching can just as easily be done by hand . . . and you will never run out of bobbin. If you do have a machine and plan to use it for creating Paper Festooning (page 15), you should outfit it with a pleating foot to make it go super fast. If hand sewing, all that will be needed is a standard pack of hand sewing needles in sizes you're comfortable using.

In addition to the aforementioned tools, every craft table should have the following basic necessities:

★ Stapler
★ Ruler
★ Dressmaker's measuring tape
★ Standard #2 and colored pencils
★ Pencil sharpener

Tools

BASIC TECHNIQUES

In addition to having basic materials and tools, it's good to develop a few basic techniques that you can rely on when starting a new project. So, here are a few how-tos for skills and processes used multiple times throughout this book.

How to Make a 9-inch Cone

The size of your cone is determined by the size of the circle you start with. You can make a cone any size by adjusting the diameter of the circle to be equal to twice the height of the finished cone you want. Example: If you want a cone that is 6 inches tall, you should start with a 12-inch-diameter circle.

Materials
- ★ Poster board
- ★ White glue

Tools
- ★ Pencil
- ★ Scissors
- ★ Paintbrush

1. Draw an 18-inch-diameter circle on a piece of poster board.
2. Use scissors to cut out the circle.
3. Fold the circle in half and crease.
4. Using scissors, cut along the crease. You will now have two half-circles that are the same size. Set one aside for another use.
5. With the straight side facing up, roll the half circle into a cone shape, keeping the bottom edge as even as possible.
6. Brush the seam edge with white glue and press together.

How to Paint and Stripe a Wire

Wires can be painted in any color combination you choose, and many of the projects in this book call for painted wires.

Materials
* Floral stem wire
* White floral tape
* Acrylic paints

Tools
* Paintbrush

1. Beginning at the top of the floral stem wire, fold the end of the floral tape around at a slight angle and hold with your fingers.
2. Twist the wire in your fingers as you gently pull the floral tape in a downward motion to cover the wire as it turns. The edges of the floral tape should overlap only slightly. Be careful not to pull too hard, or the floral tape will tear.
3. Work your way to the bottom of the wire, pinch the tape at the end of the wire, and tear the floral tape.
4. Paint the covered wire with a base coat of white acrylic paint and allow to dry.
5. Using a small paintbrush, add stripes to the wire.

How to Apply Glitter

Here I am covering a party hat cone with glitter, but you can use the same techniques to cover almost anything.

Materials
* 9-inch party hat cone
* White glue
* Glitter

Tools
* Paintbrush

1. Brush a small section of the cone evenly with white glue.
2. Sprinkle glitter over the glue area. With your hand, gently press the glitter into the glue. Allow any excess glitter to fall away.
3. Continue brushing with white glue, sprinkling with glitter, and pressing in, until the entire cone is covered. Allow the glue to dry completely.

Working with Paperclay

Materials
- ★ Paperclay
- ★ Small bowl of water

Tools
- ★ Sealable plastic bag
- ★ Damp paper towel (optional)
- ★ 220-grit sandpaper

1. After opening a package of Paperclay, it's important to keep what is not being used immediately in a sealable plastic bag. This will keep the clay moist and easy to work with. If the clay becomes too soft, remove it from the bag for a short time; if it becomes too hard, put it back into the plastic bag along with a damp paper towel.
2. The biggest trick to working with Paperclay is dipping your fingers into a small bowl of water throughout the sculpting process for smoothing the clay. Sometimes an area you're sculpting will become sticky if dampened too much. If this happens, just give it a couple of minutes and it will be ready to continue.
3. When your finished sculpture has had time to dry and harden, use a 220-grit sandpaper to lightly buff its surface until smooth.

How to Paint a Face

Materials
- ★ Acrylic paint

Tools
- ★ Paintbrushes

1. Although each face is uniquely different, I generally start by painting the entire face with the base color I want the face to be.
2. Next I use a process that I call Color Blocking, which simply means to paint areas such as the eyes and mouth with a solid color.
3. Then, with a fine brush, continue with shading and adding the final details, such as the pupils and eyelashes, teeth, and other characteristics, such as warts, and so on.

Techniques

Cellophane Fancies

I must admit
that my love never wanes
for candies wrapped
in cellophane!

These tiny fancies
are the perfect surprise,
so hold out your hands,
and close your eyes.

Okay, open up,
it's there in your palm.
I know it's exciting
but you must remain calm.

There's a skeleton man,
a cat named Clancy,
and a dapper pumpkin—
yes, they are fancy!

Now untie the ribbon
and take off the wrapping.
It's filled with goodies
for keeping or passing.

I have to say
it's a beautiful treat,
for loving and holding
or even to eat.

But my little fancy
shall not be untied.
Its contents will always
be kept safe inside.

Materials

1¾-inch-diameter cardboard tube	Chenille stems in black and white
White glue	Adhesive dots
Small piece of flat cardboard	9 x 9-inch piece of cellophane
Acrylic paints	Candy to fill the cup
¾-inch-diameter wooden craft ball	Curling ribbon

Tools

Ruler	Paintbrushes
Pencil	Drill with ¹⁄₁₆-inch bit
Scissors	Pinking shears
Craft knife	

Clancy the Cat Cellophane Fancy

When I think of an elegant affair, my mind automatically imagines fancy favors tied up in cellophane with frazzled chenille characters holding on for dear life. No longer is that a treat reserved for the elite, because now we can make our own!

1 Measure ¾ inch on the cardboard tube and use a pencil to mark all the way around.

2 Cut on the marked line with scissors or a craft knife. Cutting around a tube is not always precise, but you can straighten it later if needed.

3 Apply white glue around one edge of the cardboard tube. Putting glue on just the edge is a little like making it walk a tightwire, so if it decides to run down the sides, wipe it off.

4 Stick the tube to a flat piece of cardboard and allow it to dry completely.

5 Trim carefully around the bottom edge with scissors or a craft knife. This cut is pretty important. It's the bottom of your container, so take your time.

6 Paint the cup inside and out with white acrylic paint. For this step you could also use gesso.

7 Stripe the sides with black acrylic paint and set aside to dry.

Make all the candy containers you will need before moving on to the next step.

8 Drill a hole approximately ¼ inch deep into the wooden craft ball. Insert a chenille stem to temporarily hold the ball while you paint.

9 Paint the ball with a base coat of black acrylic paint and allow to dry. It usually takes a couple of coats to get an even finish, so repeat as necessary, letting the paint dry completely before moving on.

10 Paint the details of the face, either using the photos as your guide or making your own spooky faces. Painting the features in large blocks of color helps establish feature placement and allows you to create your look in layers. Allow to dry.

11 Drill a small hole approximately ⅛ inch deep on each side at the top of the head where the ears will go. The cat's ears give him a lot of character, so pay attention to placement. Do they point straight up, or to the sides?

12 Make the ears from small (approximately ¾-inch) pieces of chenille and insert into the holes. Bend his ears to reflect his mood. Size will also affect his attitude.

13 Remove your temporary chenille stem and place the completed head onto a chenille stem body that is approximately 3 inches long.

14 Wrap another chenille stem around the center of the body to make the arms. Wrap each half of the chenille over and around the body once to keep it from sliding up and down the body.

15 To make a bow tie, fold a small chenille stem into a figure-eight shape. Attach the bow tie by bending it around the neck and cutting off the excess.

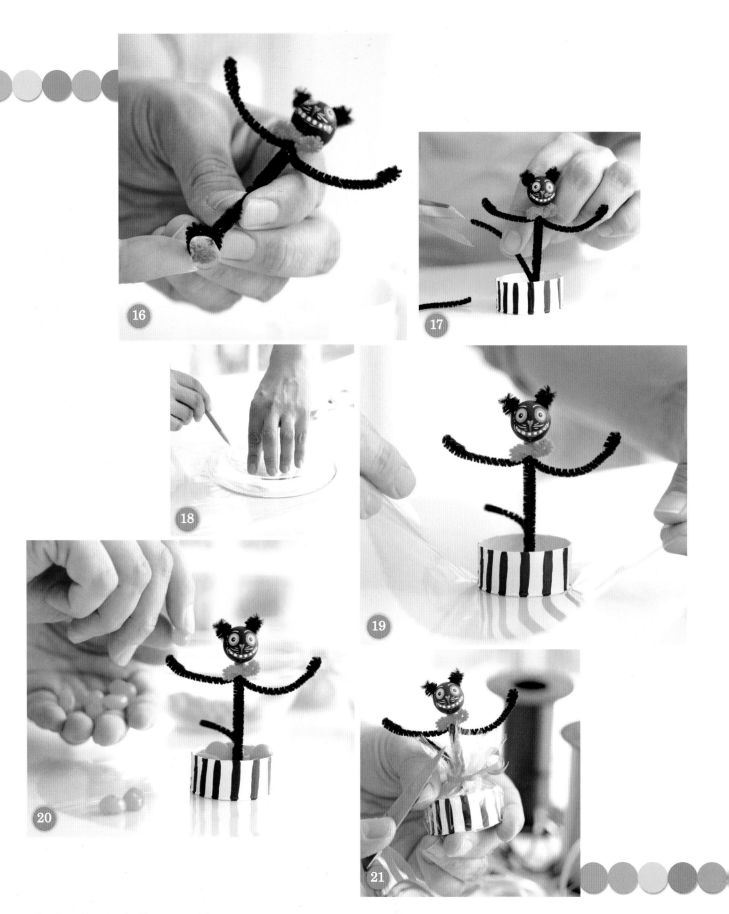

8 Return the painted, glittered card stock to the inside of the bucket. Use the scissors or craft knife to trim any card stock that interferes with the handles or is visible above the rim of the bucket. Make sure the features line up, then glue the card stock into place.

9 Paint the finishing details onto the bucket and allow to dry.

10 Wrap the wire with floral tape.

11 Paint and stripe the wire and allow to dry.

12 Insert the painted wire handle through the holes on each side of the bucket and twist to secure.

PAPER
Festooning

I'll always remember
at Halloween swooning
for anything trimmed
with paper festooning.

For your own festive crepe
to the store you may go,
but you will quickly find out
that to have, you must sew.

Whether you make it
on the machine, or even by hand,
I think you'll agree
the results are quite grand!

Use it on a wicked party hat
or as a tutu on a dancing rat!
The bottom line is simply this:
It's a project that you cannot miss.

So find a needle,
its threading looming,
and start preparing
your festooning.

Materials

Rolls of crepe paper	Coordinating thread

Tools

Pinking shears	Sewing needle
Scissors	Sewing machine
Straight pins	with a pleating foot
	(optional)

Paper Festooning

Turning ordinary crepe paper into rolls of ruffled trim is easy with a little sewing and gathering. While this may not seem like the most exciting project in the book, it is one of the most important because of its frequent use as a material in many of the other projects, such as party hats and nut cup favors. In addition to being useful, it's lovely to look at all stacked up in a pile.

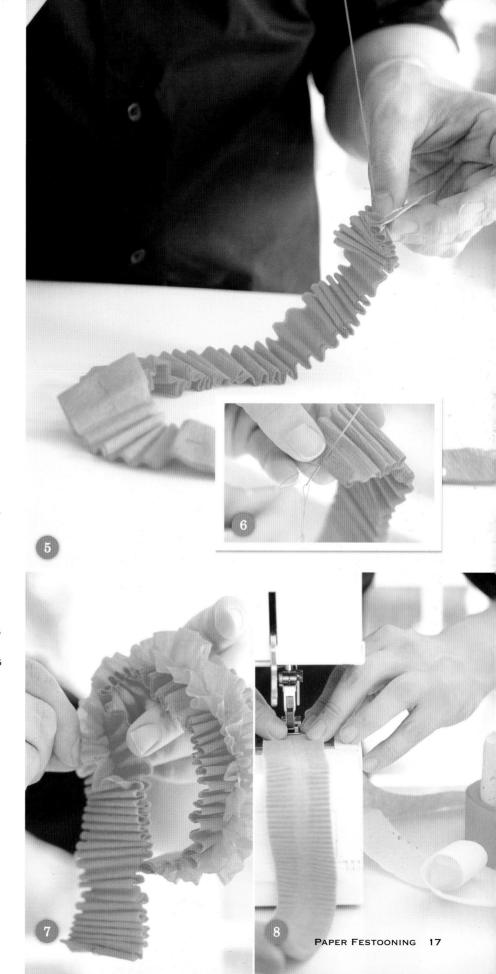

1 Begin by layering four long pieces of crepe paper. Use two different colors and alternate. Sewing will shorten the length of your original crepe paper strips, so determine how much you need and double that length before sewing.

2 Straighten out all the layers, then trim all the pieces to the same length with pinking shears or scissors and pin together at one end. You should have four pieces of crepe paper that are the same length, pinned together at one end. Now you're ready to start sewing.

3 At the end with the straight pin, tie the thread tail around the pin to anchor it.

4 Start by straight stitching down the center of the crepe paper, pulling the thread to gather the paper toward the end with the secured straight pin, while pulling the thread at the other end.

5 Continue to stitch and gather the entire length of paper slowly and carefully so that you don't tear the paper.

6 When you have gathered the paper evenly and have a piece of festooning the length desired, make a small fold, then stitch to secure the end and tie off the thread.

7 Finish by gently separating the layers and fanning them out with your fingers. Sometimes the crepe paper sticks together within the folds, which makes it hard to separate. If this happens, try separating it with a straight pin or toothpick.

8 If you have a sewing machine and a pleating foot, you can quickly make whole rolls of festooning. Layer up your crepe paper as described for hand sewing and set your machine to the longest stitch setting. Match the bobbin to the bottom paper color and the top thread to the top paper color. Sew down the center. The pleating foot will gather the paper as you sew.

Oh-So Wicked!

Party Hat

Look up to the sky
and across the moon,
see a sparkling beauty
riding a broom.

Her skin is olive,
or should I say green,
like that you would find
in pistachio ice cream.

Her glittery gown
is as black as a cat,
silhouetted like that
of a partying hat.

Her hemline is trimmed
in bat belly fur,
with a collar to match,
designed just for her.

The stars that surround her,
light up the night,
trailing behind
like the tail of a kite.

On Halloween Eve
she sprinkles her spell,
holding a banner
that's telling her tale.

Materials

White poster board

Party Hat pattern (page 168)

Acrylic paints

White glue

Black glitter

4 feet of ½-inch ribbon, preferably satin

Hot glue

Paper Festooning (page 15)

Marabou

Kitchen skewers

Card stock in assorted colors, for the stars

18-gauge floral stem wire

White floral tape (optional)

1½-inch-diameter Styrofoam ball

Paper clay

Toothpicks

Cape Pattern (page 169)

Pink card stock

Chenille stems in black

Orange card stock

Witch Hat Pattern (page 168)

Banner Art (page 168)

Tools

Paintbrushes

Hole punch

Pencil

Scissors

Ruler

Wire cutters

Star punch

Clay sculpting tool

Quilling tool (optional)

Photocopier

Craft knife

Hot glue gun

Oh-So-Wicked! Party Hat

Pay no attention to its warning of wickedness—this witchey-poo is all fun for you! Partygoers will assume you hopped a broom to Paris for this special Halloween hat, but will turn green with envy when they hear it was simple make-and-do magic. And party hats are not only for wearing—they make great centerpieces and tree toppers, too!

1 Start with four bump chenille stems. Use wire cutters to cut them apart halfway between each bump. This will give you a total of sixteen bumps.

2 Gather eight bumps together at their ends.

3 Wrap a small piece of wire around the ends to secure them together. This will end up inside the pumpkin when complete.

4 One at a time, bend the bumps up to resemble the sections of a pumpkin.

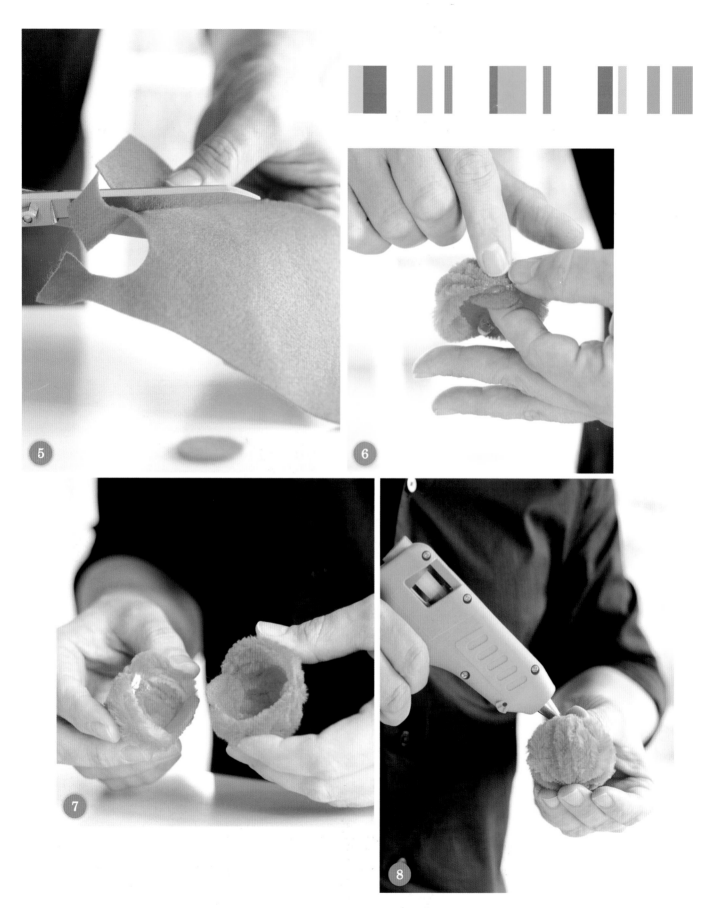

5 Cut two 1-inch-diameter circles of orange felt.

6 Hot glue the eight loose ends onto one of the felt circles. This will give you half of the pumpkin.

7 Repeat steps 2 through 6 with the other eight bumps. Now you have two identical halves.

8 Put the halves together with both of the felt ends at the top. Hot glue at the top and bottom. It should now look like a whole pumpkin.

9 Cut out felt eyes, a nose, and a mouth. Use white or hot glue to attach them to the side of the pumpkin.

10 Make the pumpkin stem and vine by wrapping a brown chenille stem around a toothpick and a green chenille stem around a marker or similarly-sized object.

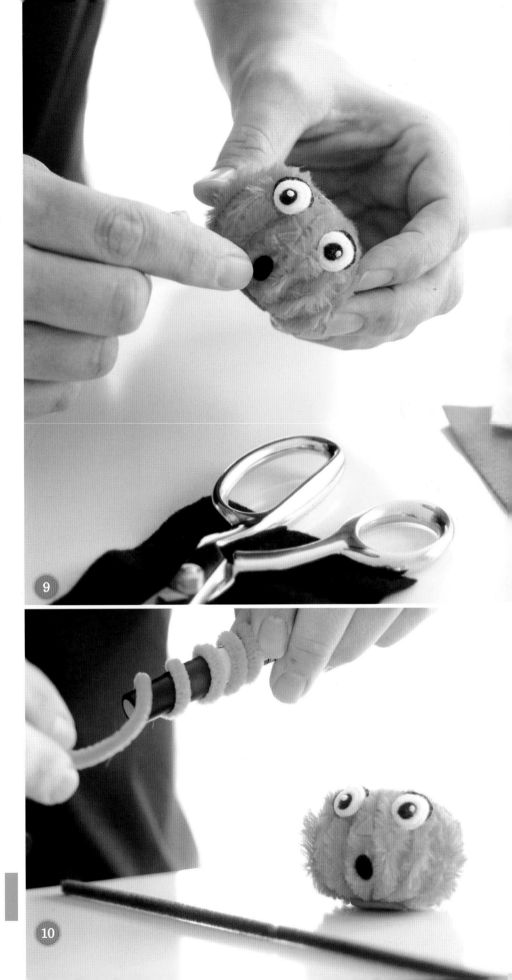

9

10

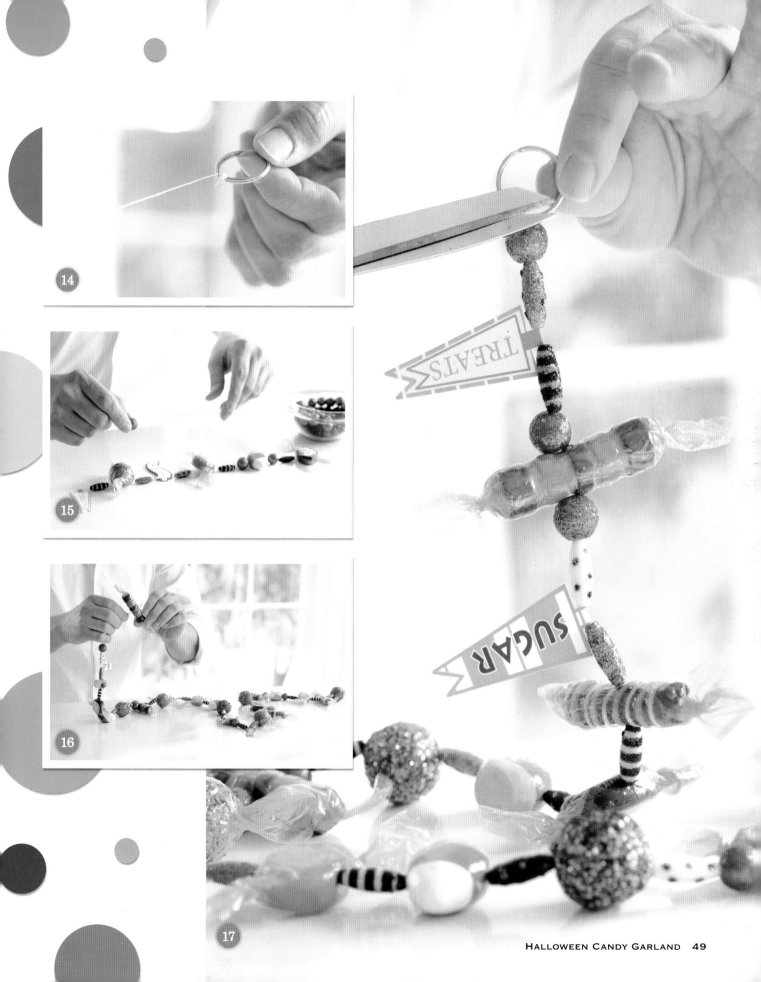

ButterScream FROSTING
Ornament

It's Halloween, and here's the plan
I'm going to bake a cupcake man,
made from butter, sugar, and flour,
shoved into the oven for almost an hour.

"Ding" goes the timer, and now he must cool.
He's too hot for frosting, so waiting's the rule.
His wrapper's filled with chocolate cake,
and now his frosting I must make.

As I stood there quickly whipping,
my cooling timer started beeping,
but when I turned I got a huge surprise—
my cupcake man had begun to rise.

When I say rise, I really mean walking,
standing before me, blinking and talking.
He said, "Today is my birthday, and it's Halloween.
Make me spooky and sweet for the new candy scene."

So I frosted his top, swirled up with a peak
and then ready was he for a trick and a treat.
He said, "I'm not scary if costumed in sweet buttercream."
Well, "Of course not," said I, "you're frosted in boo butter scream!"

MAKE AND DO! GATHER YOUR GLITTER, SCISSORS AND GLUE, HERE'S EVERYTHING NEEDED FOR THIS

Materials

3-inch by 2-inch Styrofoam cone

2-inch-diameter Styrofoam ball

Toothpicks

Paperclay

18-inch piece of 16-gauge floral stem wire

Floral tape

Acrylic paint

White glue

Mask Pattern (page 170)

Thread

1-inch-diameter Styrofoam ball

18-gauge floral stem wire

6-inch piece of ⅛-inch satin ribbon for hanging

Tools

Serrated knife

Ruler

Wire cutters

New #2 pencil with eraser (optional)

Clay sculpting tool

Paintbrushes

Drill with ¹⁄₁₆-inch bit

Needle-nose pliers

Pencil for tracing

Scissors

Craft knife

Large sewing needle

ButterScream Frosting Ornament

This yummy cupcake is all dressed up and looking for treats! But instead of the sugar and flour that's needed for baking, you will use clay for this cupcake's making! Now if you're like me, you can't make just one, so do a baker's dozen for added fun!

1   With a serrated knife, cut approximately 1 inch from the top and ½ inch from the bottom of the Styrofoam cone. This will be the base of your cupcake. These measurements are pretty specific for the materials I'm using, but you can basically just cut a Styrofoam cone to be the size you want your cupcake to be.

2   Cut the 2-inch Styrofoam ball in half with the serrated knife. This will be the icing on your cupcake.

3   Place the frosting on top of the base as shown and push in toothpicks to hold them together.

4   Use wire cutters to trim the toothpicks even with the Styrofoam.

5   With the end of a pencil, make indentations in the Styrofoam for the eyes. The eraser end of a brand-new #2 pencil is perfect for making round eye indentions.

6   With the side of the pencil, make indentations in the Styrofoam for the mouth.

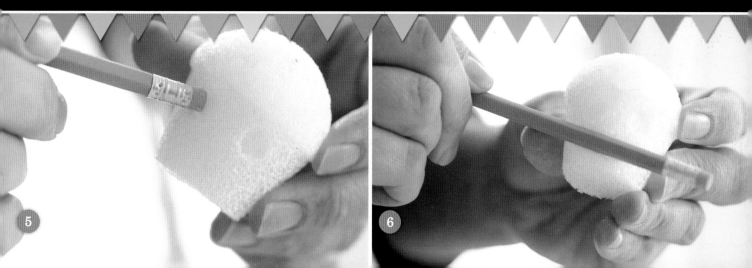

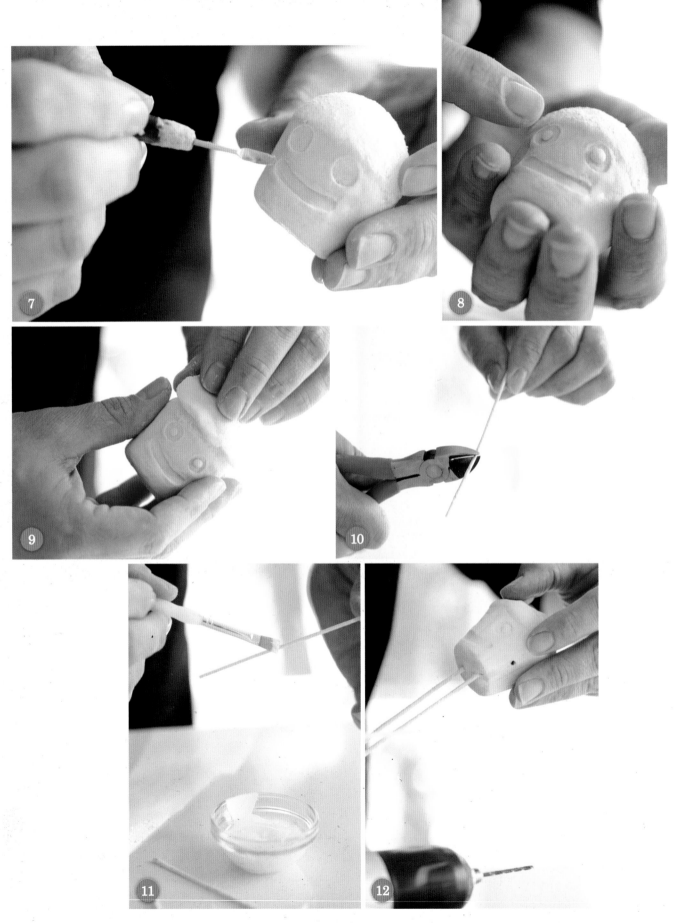

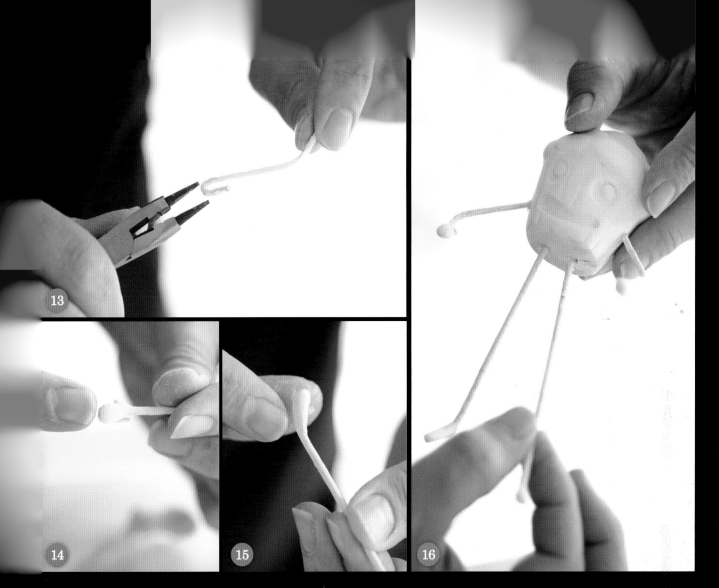

7 Make a roll of paperclay and then flatten it into a rectangle. Apply this to the sides of the cupcake base, pressing the clay into the indentations for the eyes and mouth. Smooth and blend with your fingers or sculpting tool.

8 Add two small balls of paperclay to the eye indentations for pupils. Remember to wet them before adding, to ensure that they stick.

9 Add balls of paperclay to the top. Shape and smooth to form the icing on your cupcake. Set the cupcake aside to allow the paperclay to harden.

10 Cover the 18-inch piece of 16-gauge wire with floral tape and cut two 3½-inch pieces for the arms and two 4½-inch pieces for the legs.

11 Paint the wires with a base coat of white and allow to dry.

12 Drill four holes in the cupcake (approximately ½ inch deep), insert the arms and legs, and bend into shape. Do not glue the arms or legs in yet; we're just trying them on for size!

13 At the end of the left arm, use a pair of needle-nose pliers to turn under a small loop. This is where the candy bucket will hang.

14 Add balls of paperclay to the ends of the arm wires and shape them into hands. Make sure to leave the wire loop open and exposed behind the left hand.

15 Add balls of paperclay to the ends of the leg wires and shape them into feet. Don't stress about the technical difficulties of making realistic feet. Simplify your sculpting and add the details with paint.

16 Use white glue to secure the arms and legs.

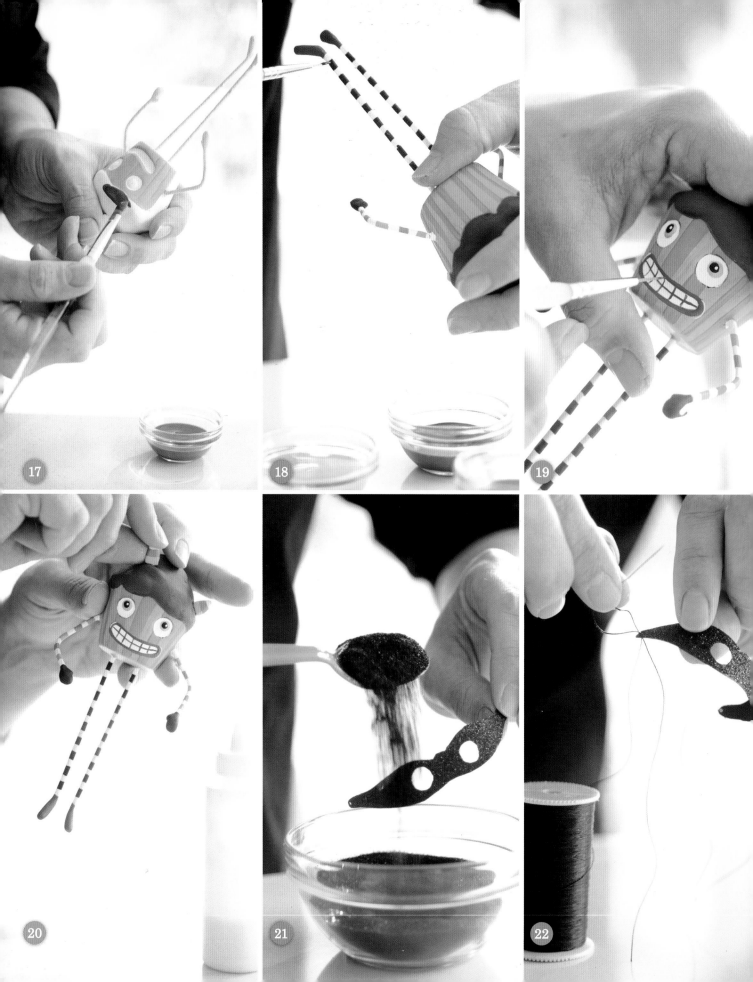

17 Paint a base coat and color block on the cupcake and frosting, including the eyes and mouth. Allow to dry.

18 Add stripes to the arms, legs, and cupcake.

19 Paint the details of the face.

20 Make small candy corn shapes from paperclay. Once they are hardened, paint them to look like candy corn and glue to the frosting on top of the cupcake.

21 Trace the mask pattern onto card stock and use scissors or a craft knife to cut it out. Paint it black and add glitter.

22 Make tiny holes in the ends of the mask with a large needle and use thread to tie it onto the cupcake.

23 Trim excess thread.

23

24 For the treat bucket, cut the top off the 1-inch Styrofoam ball. Press in the center of the flat side with your fingers. This will be the top of the bucket.

25 Cover with paperclay; shape and smooth. Bend the 18-gauge wire to shape the handle, then insert it into the ball.

26 Add tiny pieces of paperclay candy to the bucket, then set aside to harden.

27 Paint the bucket and allow to dry.

28 Attach the treat bucket by hanging it on the upturned wire behind the left hand. Secure it by gently closing the loop with needle-nose pliers.

29 Drill a hole in the top of the cupcake figure and glue in a bent-wire hanging loop. Finish off with a ribbon for tying.

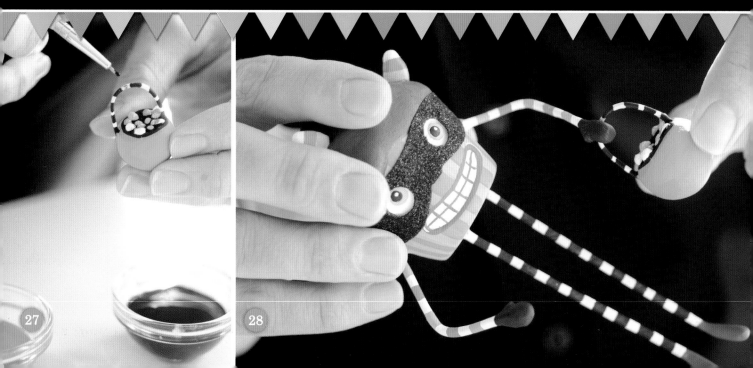

Nut CUPS

I once had a party
and hired squirrels to hold nuts,
and while this seems sensible,
it comes with a but . . .

Fanciful? Yes,
that much is true,
but what a commotion!
What are we to do?

Well . . . there's a party favor,
gala-goers do savor.
It's a small paper cup
that's filled up with nuts.

But the memories of squirrels
have me so forlorn,
that this year I'm filling them
with sweet candy corn.

Materials

Clip Art (page 171)
White card stock
White glue or hot glue

Paper Festooning (page 15) in various colors, or marabou

Chenille stems

Candy or nuts to fill the cups

Tools

Printer
Scissors

Craft knife
Ruler

Nut Cups

One of my favorite Halloween projects is making my own version of traditional nut cup favors. These miniature paper baskets have been popular on party tables since the early 1900s, and although the name sounds quite specific, filling the cup with candies is also terrific. Party guests love a goodie to go, so I always place a stacking cake plate near the door, filled with nut cups for picking up as they leave.

1

8 Paint the ball with a pink base coat and allow to dry.

9 Use a pencil to lightly sketch the features of the face.

10 Color block the eyes, nose, and mouth with white paint.

11 Add orange shading around the eyes, nose, and mouth, as well as around the sides, to define the segments of the pumpkin. Allow to dry.

12 Paint the details of the eyes.

13 Finish the painted details of the nose and mouth.

14 You can add even more details with colored pencils and a #2 pencil.

15 Remove the skewer (if it's already tight just leave it), brush the end with white glue, and insert it back into the pumpkin to make the stem.

16 Dip the end of a regular chenille stem in white glue, stick it to the base of the skewer and wrap it up and around two to three times. Leave the tail for now.

17 Use wire cutters to cut the skewer where the chenille wrapping ends.

18 Create a hanger for the pumpkin by making a loop and wrapping the tail back around the pumpkin stem. Cut off any excess with wire cutters. Wrap a piece of small chenille stem (approximately 3 inches long) around a toothpick to form a corkscrew shape and attach it to the pumpkin stem by bending it around.

19 Apply a little white glue to the eyes, nose, and mouth and add glitter to make your pumpkin sparkle.

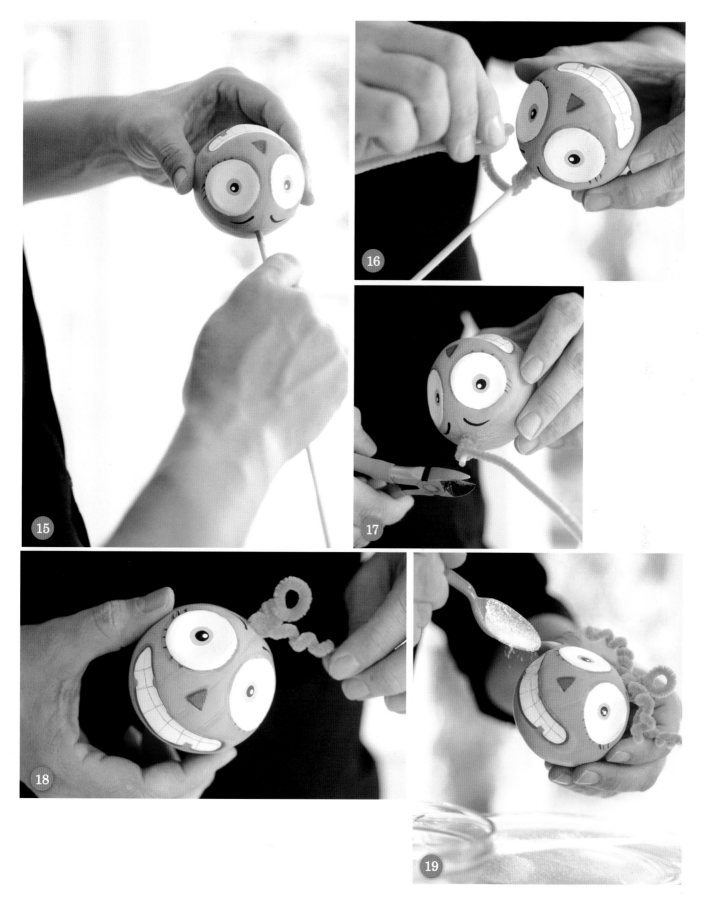

Wacky Willie Webber
SPIDER PUPPET

Most spiders spin webs of silk and string,
for catching flies and buzzing things.
But Willie Webber's web is wacky.
It's completely made from taffy.

His hanging home
is eight legs pulled,
with skills he learned
in candy school.

He's trying a new recipe
for everyone to come and see,
What will this pink confection be?
I do not know—enlighten me!

He had it at a carnival
and never has forgotten
a wad of webs around a stick,
just like a candy cotton.

With four arms out
and four arms in,
he made the thread
like sugar spin.

In less time than saying "Yankee doodle,"
he made a cotton candy poodle.
If you are near, by his web you should drop
it's now called Willie's Candy Shop.

If you come visit, hungry, hoping,
but it's evening, are they open?
However your cravings flow and ebb,
Willie's 24/7 on the web.

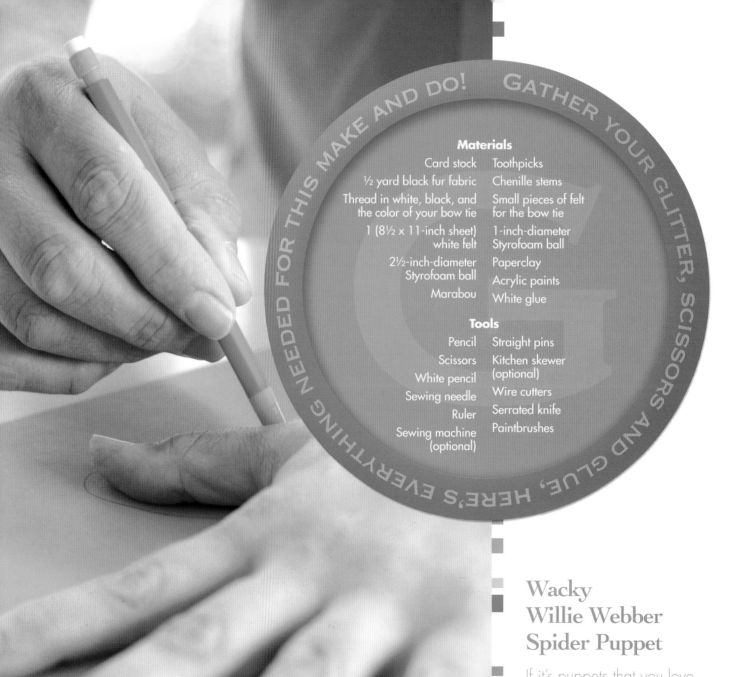

Materials

Card stock	Toothpicks
½ yard black fur fabric	Chenille stems
Thread in white, black, and the color of your bow tie	Small pieces of felt for the bow tie
1 (8½ x 11-inch sheet) white felt	1-inch-diameter Styrofoam ball
2½-inch-diameter Styrofoam ball	Paperclay
	Acrylic paints
Marabou	White glue

Tools

Pencil	Straight pins
Scissors	Kitchen skewer (optional)
White pencil	Wire cutters
Sewing needle	Serrated knife
Ruler	Paintbrushes
Sewing machine (optional)	

Wacky Willie Webber Spider Puppet

If it's puppets that you love, this project will fit you like a glove—literally! This project is so easy that it doesn't even require a pattern, just your hand! I remember the year I dressed as a web and wore a spider puppet on one hand and carried my candy bucket with the other, which was great fun but made scratching my nose almost impossible.

1 Create a pattern by tracing your hand with a pencil on a piece of card stock.

2 Draw another line approximately ¼ inch larger than your hand tracing. This will be the line you follow when sewing together.

3 Use sharp scissors to cut out the pattern.

4 Place the pattern on the wrong side of a piece of black fur fabric. Make sure the stretch of the fabric (the grain) is going across the palm of the hand. Trace around the pattern with a white pencil.

5 Flip the pattern over and trace the second half of the glove body. Set this piece aside for now.

6 Cut out both pieces loosely around the traced hand shapes. Use white thread to hand stitch around the outline on the top piece of the glove. This is just a marking thread and is not meant to hold anything together since this is only one layer of fabric.

7 Use a white pencil to draw the location of the stripes across the fingers on the wrong side of the fur, then hand stitch loosely along the lines with white thread. When we turn the fabric over to apply stripes we will easily see our white threads for placement.

8 Cut 15 strips of white felt approximately ½ inch wide and long enough to fit across each finger of your glove.

9 Using the white stitches as a guide, place the strips of white felt on the RIGHT SIDE of the fur on the top of your glove. Sew both edges of each stripe with a sewing machine (or hand stitch if you don't have a machine).

10 Place the two glove pieces right sides together and pin. Sew along the white guideline with black thread all the way around.

11 Using sharp scissors, carefully clip between the fingers with scissors and trim close to the stitches. Now you have a glove.

12 Turn the glove right side out. A kitchen skewer makes this easier, but be careful not to poke a hole through your material.

13 For the spider's head, cut a piece of fur 8¼ x 4½ inches. Wrap around a 2½-inch Styrofoam ball.

14 With a needle and black thread, hand sew the fabric onto the ball.

15 Run a gathering stitch around the side opening and pull the thread to close. Knot and repeat on the other side.

16 Attach the head to the glove by hand stitching. Stitch a piece of marabou around the neck.

12

13

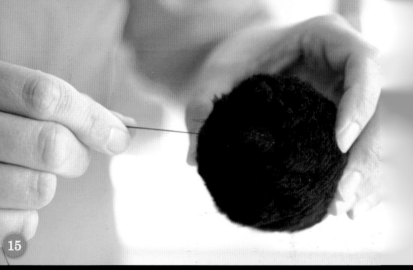

15

14

16

17 Make two holes in the top of the head with a toothpick. Use wire cutters to cut two chenille stem antennae about 6 inches long. Curl them and insert them into the holes. Cut another piece of chenille stem about 6 inches long, bend it into shape for the mouth, and hand stitch it on.

18 Cut out a small bow tie from orange felt, add a pink felt center, and stitch on.

19 Make the nose by adding two small white stitches.

20 For the eyes, use a serrated knife to cut a 1-inch Styrofoam ball in half. Cover each half with paper-clay and smooth it. Push each half onto a toothpick and allow the clay to dry and harden.

21 Paint a base coat of white on each half, allow to dry, and then paint on the details. Allow to dry.

22 Stick two trimmed toothpicks through the fur into the Styrofoam ball, apply glue to the backs of each of the eyes, and push each onto a toothpick.

Use these same how to instructions to make Willy's wife Lilly or create characters of your own!

LUMBER
JACK

Some pumpkins dream of Halloween,
with candles lit, their faces seen.

But there's a pumpkin growing among the beans
who imagines twigs and trees of green.

He's very tall and slender thin
with squash fuzz whiskers on his chin.

A flannel shirt upon his back,
he wants to be a lumberjack.

With a mighty ax of candy corn
he's off to the woods, where trees are born.

Not to chop them—my goodness, no!
He wants to take one home to grow.

"I'll plant an acorn in a small striped pot
so all can see just what I've got!"

With sunshine and topsoil and water to soak,
he'll grow to be a mighty oak.

Materials

1-inch-diameter Styrofoam ball	White glue
Paperclay	Small strip of fabric or ribbon for the suspenders
Two ¼-inch-diameter dowels	Thread for the hat
Two 18-inch pieces of 16-gauge floral stem wire	Toothpicks
Floral tape	Small wooden craft flowerpot
Gesso or white acrylic paint	Five 3-inch pieces of 32-gauge wire
Fine-grade sandpaper (220 grit)	Card stock
Acrylic paints	Bump chenille stem in brown
Fabrics for the shirt, pants, and hat	Chenille stems in black and white
	Wooden craft base

Tools

Clay sculpting tool	Drill with ¹⁄₁₆- and ³⁄₃₂-inch bits
Pencil sharpener	
Ruler	Paintbrushes
Easy Cutter tool, or hacksaw (optional)	Scissors
	Sewing needle
Wire cutters	Kitchen fork
Pencil	

Lumber Jack

There is nothing I love more than spending the day at my craft table creating folk art figures. No two are alike and each one has a different personality than the one I made before. The process is the most important thing to be learned from this project, rather than trying to reproduce my figure exactly—a task that would be hard even for me.

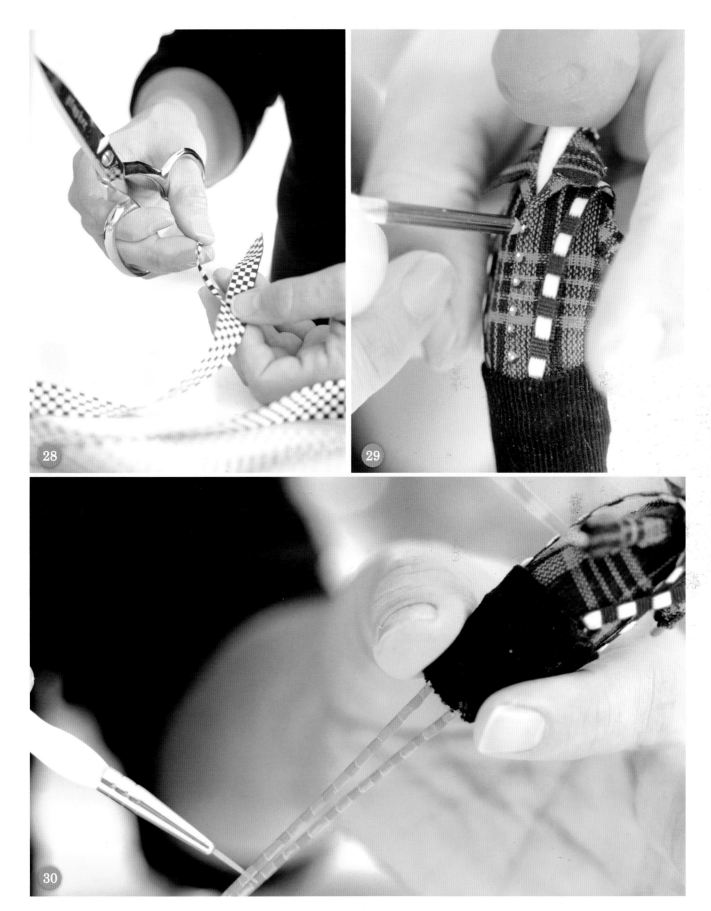

31 Bend the arms into position, attach small pieces of paperclay and shape to look like the hands, allow to harden, and paint. Don't forget to plan the shape of the hands around the accessories. In this case, he must hold an ax in one hand and a small pot in the other.

32 Make a candy corn ax by covering a toothpick with paperclay for the handle and adding a paperclay candy corn shape to the top. Paint the handle to look like faux wood and the ax like a piece of candy corn. Place the ax in his hand and secure with white glue.

33 Make a potted tree by painting a small wooden flowerpot and adding a tree made from twisting together 32-gauge wire and gluing on tiny paper leaves. Paint the tree and leaves. Use white glue to secure the potted tree in his hand.

34 Use acrylic paints to color block in the eyes, nose, and mouth.

35 Finish the face with such details as the pupils, eyelashes, eyebrows, and teeth. I've removed the head for easier access.

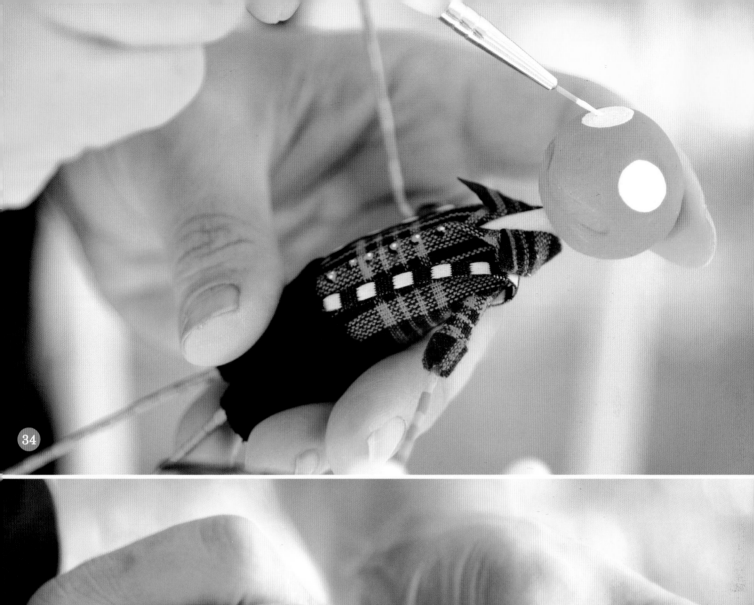

34

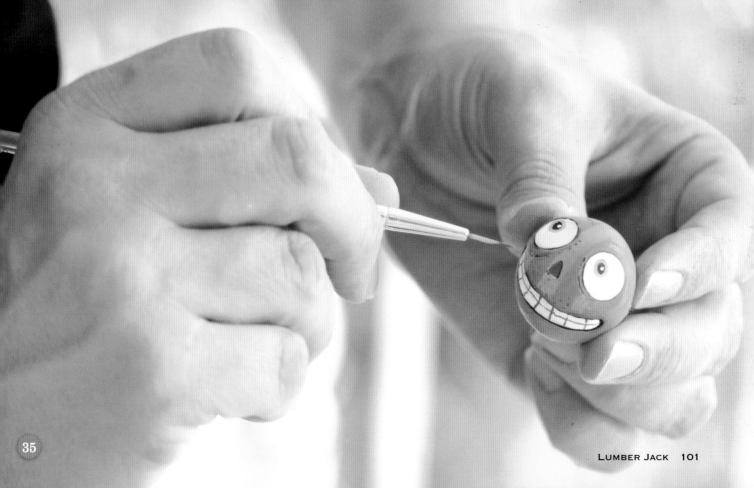

35

36 Drill small holes with a 1/16-inch bit on each side of the face for attaching the beard. Cut a small piece of bump chenille stem and insert it into the holes.

37 Cut a small rectangle of fabric for the hat and sew it together at one end.

38 Turn the bottom up to create a cuff and make a gathering stitch to close the top. Glue the hat onto the head.

39 Start with a basic wooden craft base. Moisten it with wet fingers and apply paperclay around the edge of the base. Blend and shape to look like a stump.

40 Use a kitchen fork to add bark details. Allow the paper clay to harden, then coat with gesso and allow to dry.

41 Paint the base to look like a stump.

42 Drill two holes with a 3/32-inch bit in the base to hold the figure. Attach by inserting the wires below the shoes into the holes.

43 Wrap alternating black and white chenille stems above the shoes to make striped socks. Lumber Jack complete!

Materials

Butter, for coating the baking sheet

6 medium-size apples (McIntosh apples work well)

2 cups granulated sugar

½ cup light corn syrup

Orange food coloring

¾ cup water

Tools

¼-inch-diameter kitchen skewers

Baking sheet

Heavy-bottomed saucepan

Rubber spatula (heat safe)

Candy thermometer

Orange Candy Apples

Makes 6

Candy apples are a beautiful treat that's fun to eat! Although I can't imagine not making the Spooky Forest Sticks for these, you could use this same recipe with average candy apple sticks.

1 Coat a baking sheet evenly with butter to keep the candy apples from sticking, and set aside.

2 Insert a kitchen skewer securely into each apple and set aside.

3 Place the sugar into the heavy-bottomed saucepan.

4 Add the corn syrup.

5 Add the orange food coloring to the ¾ cup water and pour into the sugar mixture.

6 Stir to combine.

7 Bring the mixture to a boil over high heat, stirring constantly.

8 Reduce the heat to medium-high and place the candy thermometer into the pan.

9 Continue stirring and checking the temperature often until the mixture reaches hard-crack stage (300° to 310°F). Don't worry—it takes a while!

10 When the temperature reaches 300° to 310°F, immediately remove the pan from the heat and set it on a heatproof work surface.

11 Dip the apples into the hot mixture one at a time, making sure to completely coat each apple. You must work quickly because the mixture will harden rapidly as it cools. Carefully place the dipped apples on the buttered baking sheet and allow to harden. Quickly place all of your candy-coated utensils into a sink full of water for easy cleanup. Otherwise, the same hard candy on your apples will form on your thermometer.

12 Carefully remove the kitchen skewers from the hardened apples and replace them with Spooky Forest Sticks.

PARTY HAT

Place Card Holders

It's time to be seated
at the party table,
though it's missing a leg
and a little unstable.

But find a place,
and make your claim,
at the tiny party hat
bearing your name.

There's a ghost and a bat
and a big black spider.
Miss Muffet is coming,
but she's not seated beside her.

Place cards give the hostess
a swell presentation,
but are really just covers
for seat manipulation.

You try to sit here,
but, oh . . . there's your name.
One quickly discovers
the name of this game.

Seating at parties
is surely an art,
but to create chatter that matters
it's definitely smart.

Materials

Card stock	Paper Festooning (page 15)
White glue	
Arms, Wings, and Legs patterns (page 172)	18-gauge floral stem wire
Acrylic paints	Banner Art (page 172)

Tools

Printer	Scissors
Pencil	Clothespin
Paintbrushes	Craft knife

Pumpkin Party Hat Place Card Holder

To entertain like you are the mostest requires planning and crafting from the host or the hostess. People are always impressed when they feel you have gone out of your way to make them feel special, and this will certainly be the case when your guests sit down at a table full of miniature party hats bearing their names.

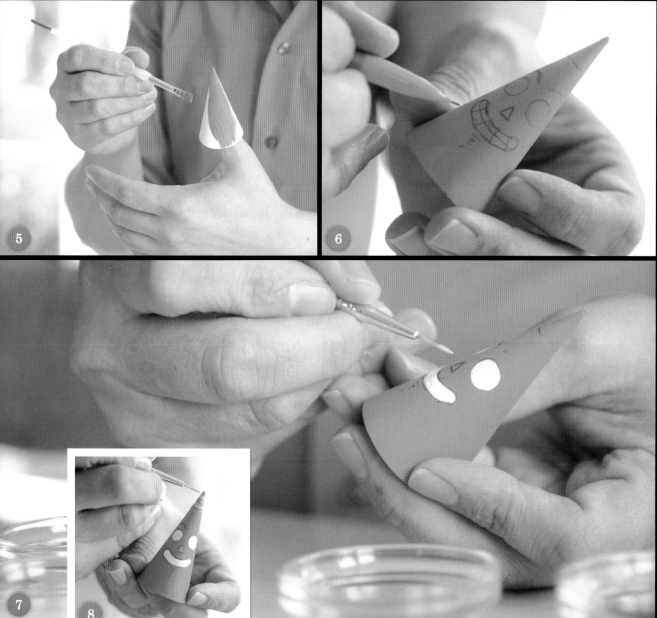

1 Trace a 6-inch-diameter half circle onto card stock. Copy the pattern for the pumpkin arms and use a pencil to trace them onto card stock.

2 Use sharp scissors to cut out the cone.

3 Cut out two arms and set aside.

4 Carefully roll the cone into shape and secure with white glue. Use a clothespin to hold it at the seam until dry. This allows you to continue making more cones.

5 Paint a base coat of orange and allow it to dry. Orange is one of those colors that never covers on the first coat, so be prepared to apply multiple coats.

6 Use a pencil to lightly sketch the face onto the cone. This allows you to erase or change the face if you want to.

7 Start the face by painting the basic features.

8 Paint the top of the cone to look like a tiny party hat wearing a party hat!

9 Use a craft knife to make a small slit on each side of the cone. Slip the arms through and secure them on the inside with glue.

10 Paint the arms and finish off the facial details.

11 Trim a piece of paper festooning on approximately ¼ inch to either side of the center stitching. This will give you a ½-inch piece of festooning. Keep the trimmings for making the hat topper later.

12 Fringe the edges by snipping with scissors.

13 Wrap the festooning around the bottom of the cone, trim to fit, then secure with white glue.

14 For the hat topper, make a small loop at the end of a piece of 18-gauge wire.

15 Roll the paper around the end of the wire and pinch it together to make the glue stick.

16 Snip the edges of the festooning with scissors.

17 Attach the hat topper by inserting the wire into the top of the cone and securing it on the inside with glue.

18 Copy the banner art on card stock and cut it out.

19 Add the name of your guest to the banner and attach to the hat with white glue.

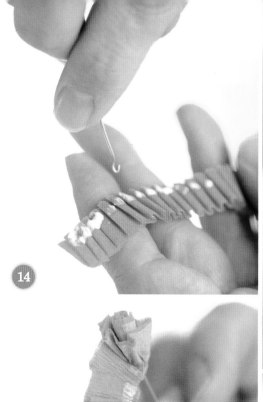

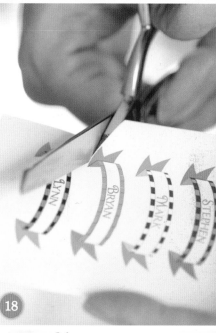

GLITTERED CAT SILHOUETTE PARTY HAT

For wearing or sharing or even decoration,
party hats instantly bring celebration.

Everyone's ready to put on a show,
when upon their head is a paper chapeau!

They're made very simply, with common things you use,
like cardboard and glitter, paints and white glue.

Lay it all out like you're a top hat designer.
The fact that you're not is a detail that's minor.

Unlike an everyday conical hat,
you don't start with a cone—they're Napoleonically flat.

So add some fun to the top of your head.
Wear it all day, and then wear it to bed!

In fact, wear it forever and don't take it off,
fun has a price and party hats are the cost!

GATHER YOUR GLITTER, SCISSORS AND GLUE, HERE'S EVERYTHING NEEDED FOR THIS MAKE AND DO!

Materials

Hat Pattern (page 173)	Red glitter for mouth
Medium-weight cardboard	Clear iridescent glitter for the eyes
Acrylic paints	Paper fasteners
White glue	Banner Art (page 175)
Orange glitter	Card stock

Tools

Pencil	Paintbrushes
Scissors	Hole punch
Craft knife	Printer

Glittered Cat Silhouette Hat

It's flat as a flitter and covered in glitter, this partying hat modified with a cat. My inspiration for this project came from popular party hats of the 1920s, worn by the gala-goers on the pages of vintage magazines. Much simpler to make than its conical shaped cousin, this hat's biggest requirements are a steady hand and a sharp craft knife.

1

1 Use a pencil to trace the hat pattern pieces onto medium weight cardboard.

2 Use scissors to cut out all the hat pieces. Use a craft knife on pattern **A** to create the silhouette.

3 Base coat pieces **A**, **B**, and **D** with black paint and allow to dry.

4 For piece **C**, paint the front orange and the back black. Allow to dry.

5 Lay the silhouette front piece **A** over the solid front piece **C** and lightly trace where the eyes, nose, and mouth of the cat are.

6 Take the pieces apart again and color block where the eyes, nose, and mouth are on piece **C**. Allow to dry.

7 Coat the area to be glittered on piece **C** with white glue, avoiding the face area.

8 Sprinkle with orange glitter and allow to dry.

9 Next, glue and glitter the facial features. Use red glitter for the mouth and clear iridescent for the eyes.

10 Brush the back of the silhouette front piece **A** with white glue.

11 Carefully line up piece **A** and **C** and press together. This is the completed front piece for the hat. Allow to dry.

12 Paint the final details on the cat's face and hat.

13 Stack the completed front piece **A** and piece **B** on top of each other. Punch holes where

indicated at the sides. Punch holes in two of the stars. You should still have two star shapes without holes that will be used later.

14 Insert a paper fastener through each of the stars with holes and through the holes on the sides of the hat from the back to the front, then bend to secure. The open legs of the paper fasteners will be on the front.

1 Use a serrated knife to cut the Styrofoam ball in half.

2 Brush the round side of the half-ball with white glue and press a 6-inch square of aluminum foil over it, leaving the excess foil flat around the half-ball as shown. Covering Styrofoam with foil makes it seem more substantial and allows it to accept glitter much more evenly.

3 Turn the half-ball over, brush the flat side with white glue, and add another 6-inch square of foil as shown.

4 Use scissors to trim the excess foil, leaving about ¼ inch all the way around.

5 Use your fingers to fold the foil toward the flat area of the half-ball all the way around. This will be easier if you snip the edges before folding.

6 Paint the rounded side of the half-ball black and allow to dry.

7 Brush the rounded part of the half-ball with white glue and sprinkle it with glitter. Do not glitter the flat side.

8 Make a pleated circle of crepe paper and use flat-headed straight pins to secure it to the flat side of the half-ball.

9 Use pinking shears to cut a black felt circle that is approximately 2 inches in diameter.

10 Use hot glue to attach the felt circle to the center of the pleated crepe paper, making sure the straight pins are hidden underneath.

11 Sculpt the moon medallion for the front of the ornament out of paperclay and allow it to harden.

12 Paint the medallion with a base coat of yellow and allow to dry.

13 Color block the eyes, nose, and mouth and allow to dry.

14 Paint the finishing details and allow to dry.

15 Brush the moon face with white glue and sprinkle with clear iridescent glitter.

16 Hot glue the finished medallion in the center of the felt circle. I've also added a small paperclay rocket.

17 Use a kitchen skewer to make a small hole in the top of the ornament.

18 Make a small loop for hanging out of a 3-inch piece of regular chenille stem. Dip the ends in white glue and insert them into the hole on the top of the ornament.

kooky
CUPCAKE
PICKS

Make your cupcakes
extra kooky,
with these picks,
so cute and spooky.

In every little bakery treat
should be these decorations sweet.
Standing tall above the frosting,
made for keeping, not for tossing.

Start with dingy the bat,
which is the one I like most,
then design your own,
like Googles the ghost.

Your new creations
will bring a huge hooray,
when people see
this party pick display!

1

EVERYTHING NEEDED FOR THIS MAKE AND DO! GATHER YOUR GLITTER, SCISSORS AND GLUE. HERE'S EVERYTHING

Materials

1-inch-diameter Styrofoam ball	White glue
Paperclay	Acrylic paints
Toothpick	9-inch piece of 16-gauge floral stem wire
Wing and Ear Patterns (page 176)	Floral tape
Card stock	Banner Art (page 176)

Tools

Clay sculpting tool	Craft knife
Pencil	Paintbrushes
Scissors	Printer

Bat Kooky Cupcake Pick

Make your cupcakes extra kooky with these frightfully fun picks. More elaborate than those plastic ones of the past, these tall totems are sure to delight party guests both young and old!

2

3

4

16 With your finger, make an indentation in the Styrofoam for the mouth.

17 Dip the cube in water to moisten each side. Wetting the Styrofoam helps the paperclay adhere better.

18 Begin by working the paperclay into the indentation of the mouth, then continue adding paper clay until the cube is completely covered.

19 Add two small flat disks of paperclay for the eyes. Blend and shape with your fingers or sculpting tool. Allow the paperclay to harden before moving on to the painting.

20 Paint the cube with a base coat of orange, let it dry, and then add the facial details.

21 Cut two pieces of green chenille stem about 3 inches long, then curl them. Drill a small hole on each side of the head and insert a stem into each hole.

22 Drill a small hole in the top of the head and insert a toothpick. This is where the hair will attach.

23 Use a serrated knife to cut off the top 3 inches of the Styrofoam cone. This will be the base for the hair.

24 Wrap the Styrofoam hair base with marabou, securing it with straight pins as you go.

25 The white hair stripes are made from two bumps from a bump chenille stem. Attach them by pushing the ends into the bottom of the marabou-covered Styrofoam and bending them up into place.

26 Push the hairpiece onto the toothpick in the top of the head and secure it with glue.

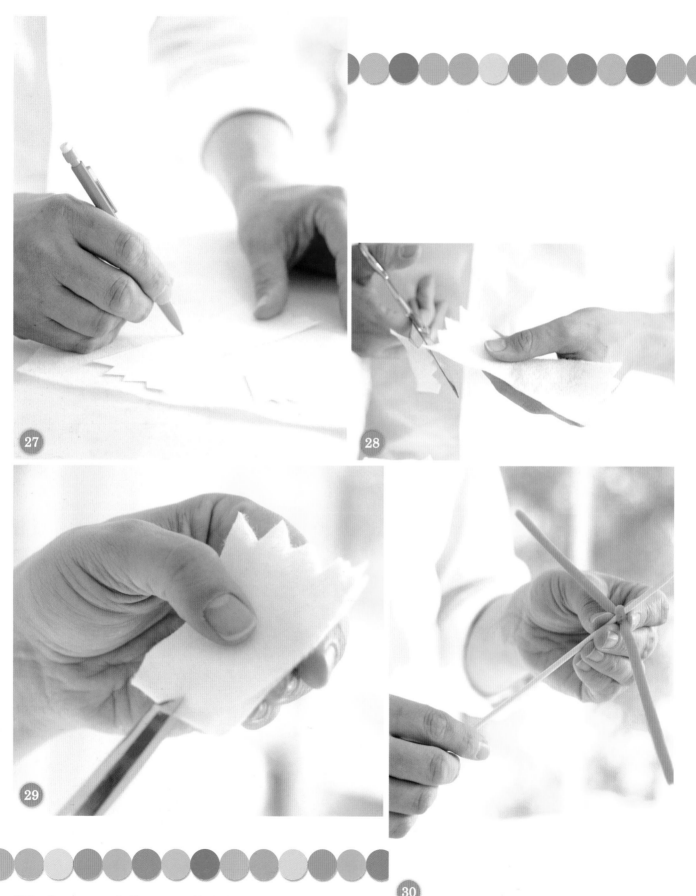

18 Add two balls of paperclay for the eyes and press gently. You want them to remain round on one side.

19 Make a small paper cone from card stock as described on page 21. Place it on top of the head and press to make a small indentation. Remove the hat and set the crow aside to allow the paperclay to dry and harden.

20 Using white glue, place the hat into the indentations on top of the crow's head. Paint the large blocks of color on the crow's body, face, and hat, and allow to dry.

21 Finish by painting the details of the face and hat. Allow to dry.

22 Position the crow in the nest and glue it into place. If you want your crow to be removable, skip this step.

23 Copy the banner art onto card stock and use sharp scissors to cut it out. Fold each letter in half and glue it onto a piece of heavy thread. Position the banner across the nest and attach it by making small loops in the ends and slipping each over a toothpick.

22

23

Oh-So-Wicked!
Party Hat

BANNER
Copy onto card stock and cut on the gray lines.
Shown Actual Size

WITCH HAT BRIM
Copy, cut out,
and trace for pattern.
Enlarge 200%

WITCH HAT CONE
Copy, cut out,
and trace for pattern.
Enlarge 200%

CAPE
Copy, cut out,
and trace for pattern.
Enlarge 200%

Candy Garland

FLAGS
Copy onto card stock
and cut out.
Shown Actual Size

ButterScream Frosting
Ornament

MASK
Copy, cut out, and trace
for pattern.
Shown Actual Size

NUT CUPS
Copy onto card stock
and cut out.
Enlarge 200%

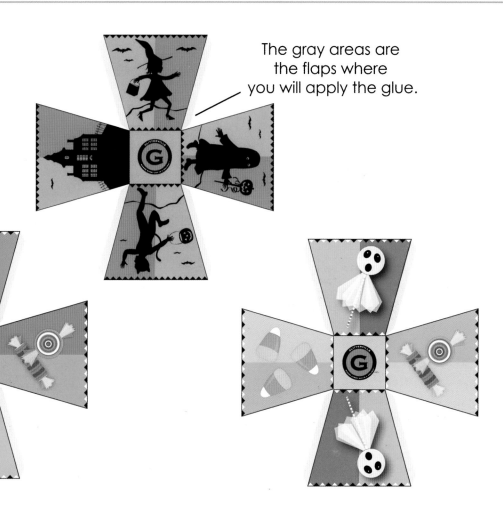

The gray areas are
the flaps where
you will apply the glue.

FLAG
Copy onto card stock and cut out.
Shown Actual Size

PATTERNS
TEMPLATES AND BANNER ART

Party Hat
Place Card Holders

BANNERS
Copy onto card stock and cut out.
Choose any color for your place card holder.
Shown Actual Size

ARMS, WINGS, LEGS
Copy, cut out,
and trace for pattern.
Shown Actual Size

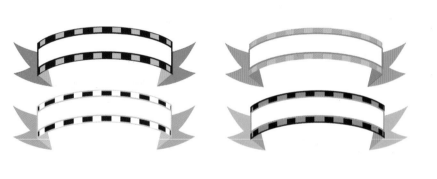

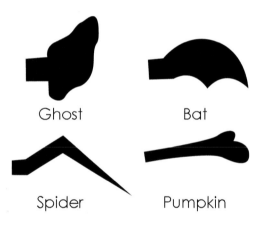

Ghost   Bat

Spider   Pumpkin

Glittered Cat Silhouette
Party Hat

STAR, Piece D
Copy, cut out,
and trace for pattern.
Enlarge 200%

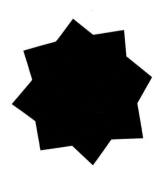

FRONT, Piece A
Copy, cut out,
and trace for pattern.
Enlarge 200%

MIDDLE, Piece B
Copy, cut out,
and trace for pattern.
Enlarge 200%

BACK, Piece C
Copy, cut out,
and trace for pattern.
Enlarge 200%

Trick or Treat

BANNER
Copy onto card stock
and cut out.
Shown Actual Size

Kooky Cupcake Picks

BANNER
Copy onto card stock and cut out.
Shown Actual Size

BAT WING & EAR
Copy, cut out, and trace for pattern.
Shown Actual Size

Pumpkin Tiara

WIRE BENDING PATTERNS
Copy or use them right out of the book.
Shown Actual Size

Attach wires to
frame at this mark.

TALL CURL
You will need
2 wires bent
in this shape.

SHORT CURL
You will need
2 wires bent
in this shape.

SIDE ARCH
You will need
2 wires bent
in this shape.

CENTER ARCH
You will need
2 wires bent
in this shape.

TIARA CROWN RIM
Copy, cut out, and trace for pattern.
Enlarge 200%

TIARA FOUNDATION WIRE
This pattern shows the size to make the foundation wire and where to attach other wire pieces.
Shown Actual Size

FLAGS
Copy onto card stock and cut out.
Shown Actual Size

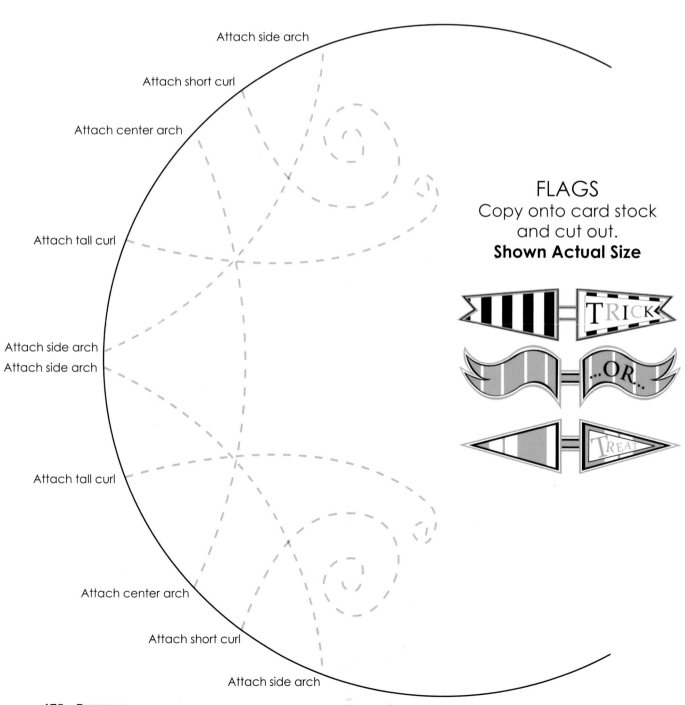

Attach side arch

Attach short curl

Attach center arch

Attach tall curl

Attach side arch
Attach side arch

Attach tall curl

Attach center arch

Attach short curl

Attach side arch

Trick or Tweet

BANNER
Copy onto card stock
and cut out.
Shown Actual Size

DRESS SLEEVES
Cut 4 pieces of felt in this shape.
Shown Actual Size

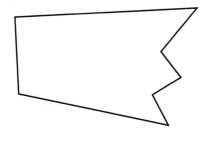

DRESS BODY
Cut 1 piece of
felt in this shape.
Shown Actual Size

BANNER
Copy onto card stock
and cut out.
Shown Actual Size

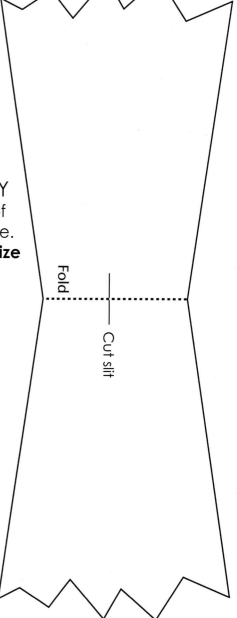

I BOO!
I BOO!
I BOO!
I BOO!

Andrews McMeel Publishing, LLC
an Andrews McMeel Universal company
1130 Walnut Street,
Kansas City, Missouri 64106

www.andrewsmcmeel.com

12 13 14 15 16 SDB 10 9 8 7 6 5 4 3 2

ISBN: 978-1-4494-1452-8

Library of Congress Control Number:
2011944594

www.glitterville.com

ATTENTION: SCHOOLS AND BUSINESSES
Andrews McMeel books are available at quantity discounts with bulk purchase for educational, business, or sales promotional use. For information, please e-mail the Andrews McMeel Publishing Special Sales Department: specialsales@amuniversal.com

THIS CRAFTING fun should never END, SO FLIP THIS BOOK OVER AND START AGAIN!